# THE BOYS' BRIGADE

## An Illustrated History

Michael A. W. Strachan

AMBERLEY

First published 2018

Amberley Publishing
The Hill, Stroud
Gloucestershire, GL5 4EP

www.amberleybooks.com

British Library Cataloguing in Publication Data.
A catalogue record for this book is available from the British Library.

ISBN 978 1 4456 7082 9 (print)
ISBN 978 1 4456 7083 6 (ebook)

Typesetting and Origination by Amberley Publishing.
Printed in Great Britain.

# Contents

Introduction                                                                    5

Chapter 1    The Founder                                                         8

Chapter 2    The Birth of a Movement                                           16

Chapter 3    The Development of Battalions                                     30

Chapter 4    The First World War – The Vindication of the BB?                  44

Chapter 5    Post-War Expansion and Union                                      54

Chapter 6    For Kings and Country                                             60

Chapter 7    Golden Age and Reorganisation                                     72

Chapter 8    Challenging Times                                                 80

Chapter 9    A Brigade for the Twenty-First Century                           85

             Conclusion                                                        92

             Bibliography                                                      96

             Acknowledgements                                                  96

# Introduction

On a weekly basis between the months of September and May, over 50,000 young people in the United Kingdom and Ireland attend meetings of the Boys' Brigade (BB). It is still one of the largest Christian organisations in Britain today, staffed by an army of 15,000 voluntary officers and leaders who dedicate their time for the furtherment of the Brigade and the young people they serve. The main goal of the organisation is to give young people a sure footing in life, and to help them achieve a personal relationship with Christ. Faith in young people is the Brigade's mission: young people are the solution, they say, not the problem.

Founded in Glasgow in 1883, the Brigade is one of the oldest Christian voluntary uniformed youth organisations in the world. The founder, Sir William Alexander Smith, produced a blueprint for boyhood that was both replicated by other organisations with similar aims, and spread around the world with the Empire. Although the Empire is gone, the footprint of the Boys' Brigade can still be seen around the world today as a testament to the strength and appeal of the original vision of a Victorian gentleman.

Since its creation, generations of boys have passed through the ranks of the Brigade, witnessing and helping to shape the rich history of the organisation that will be explored in this book. The main aim of the book is to give the reader a broad and general history of the Boys' Brigade in the United Kingdom from its founding up to the present day. It must be admitted that this book will draw most of its examples from Scotland, in particular the north of Scotland, where the author grew up in the traditions of the Brigade. It is hoped this approach may bring something new to the history of the Brigade, as it is an often-forgotten area of the BB's development in the UK.

It is sorely regretted that this history has been unable to explore the international impact of the BB around the world. So successful was the Brigade, and so hard promoted by the founder, that the Brigade was exported to almost every continent on the planet. Today there is a flourishing international Brigade family, most of which are part of the Global Fellowship, which operates in many parts of the world. The bonds are so strong, and the BB heritage shared, that even as far afield as Borneo their 'Stedfast Heritage' project is actively collecting artefacts so that they can display their history to a thriving BB community in Southeast Asia. So passionate and dedicated are these overseas entities that their histories are deserving of their own volume. It is estimated that the Brigade has more than 500,000 members worldwide.

After 135 years, the Boys' Brigade continues to offer opportunities to boys (and now girls) in building skills, physical development, gaining qualifications and developing leadership qualities. As this succinct overview of the Brigade's history will demonstrate, it is a movement that has adapted and modernised through time, allowing it to meet the needs of an ever-changing society and the needs of the young people it serves. The Brigade as we know it today, while retaining some of its traditions, would be almost unrecognisable to the Brigade of the founder. This book will chart the story of the Brigade, the changes that have occurred, and the reason for these changes.

Logo of the Boys' Brigade.

P.J.F.                    [*From a portrait by J. Finnemore, R.I.*
**Sir William A. Smith**
The Founder of the Boys' Brigade.

Sir William Alexander Smith, founder of the Boys' Brigade.

*Above*: About 1,400 BB companies still meet in church halls and public buildings around the United Kingdom. It has always been a Christian organisation, with all meeting nights starting with a Christian message and prayer.

*Right:* Logo of the Global Fellowship, which has a membership of over 500,000 around the world.

# Chapter 1

# The Founder

Far from the city streets of Glasgow that would make his name famous, the founder of the Boys' Brigade, William Alexander Smith, was born on a farm near Thurso on 27 October 1854. His birth came and went with little fanfare, other than the entry in the Kirk Register and a solitary line in the *Inverness Courier*: 'Birth – At Pennyland, Thurso, on 27th, ultimo, Mrs David Smith, of a son.'

He was born into the harsh climate of the Highlands in the almost secluded farmhouse of Pennyland, which is located between the towns of Thurso and Scrabster. On a clear day the Old Man of Hoy, Orkney, looks almost close enough to touch. Visitors to Pennyland could be excused for questioning how a man born into such humble origins went on to achieve what William Alexander Smith did. The truth of the matter is that his beginnings were anything but humble: the Smiths of Pennyland were a wealthy and influential local family who were upwardly mobile and ambitious. If the family is the first influence in life, it is clear to see how their interests shaped the ideas of young William.

The patriarch of the family was William Smith (1786–1845), who appears to have been the first Smith to occupy Pennyland. Before marriage he made his name in the military as a commissioned lieutenant in the 78th Regiment of Foot – an ancestor to the Seaforth Highlanders. It is believed that he may even have served under the Duke of Wellington in 1815. This link to the military ran down the line with his son David,

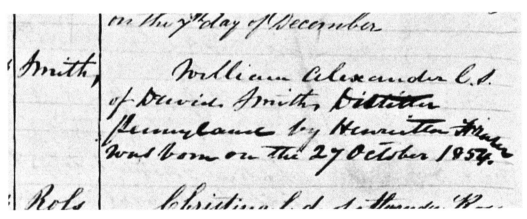

William A. Smith's baptism in the Thurso Kirk Register records his father's employment as a 'distiller'.

*Right*: Pennyland House, birthplace of the founder. (Courtesy of 1st Thurso BB)

*Below*: A plaque was erected at Pennyland House in 1950 to mark the founder's birth. (Courtesy of 1st Thurso BB)

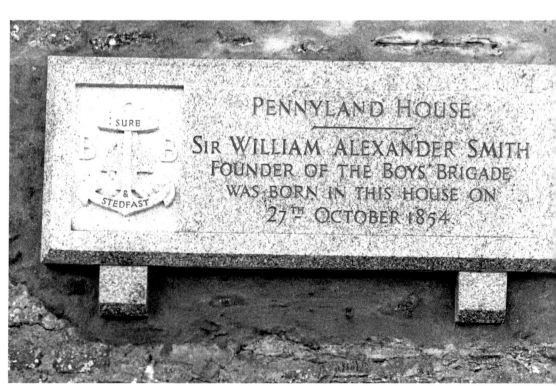

who was commissioned in to the 2nd Dragoons, and his other son, Alexander, who earned a commission with the 2nd West Indian Regiment.

Major David Smith (1823–1868), father of Sir William, continued the family's military connection with his involvement in the Thurso Volunteers. He was a keen volunteer, which would most likely have exposed his son to semi-military practises and discipline. He was extremely influential in the movement, so much so that in 1864 the annual review of the Volunteers was hosted 'in a field on the farm of Pennyland kindly granted for the purpose by Major Smith'. The Volunteers were a uniformed contingent of men participating in drill, rifle competitions and parades. It is extremely likely that a near ten-year-old William would have witnessed his father commanding these hundred men in his own back yard!

Clearly influenced by his father's activities, it was claimed that William set up a company of boys for drill and discipline in Thurso in 1865 when he was eleven. According to F. P. Gibbon's widely read history, 'About a score of boys joined; and a veteran Sergeant of the Artillery Volunteers accepted with enthusiasm the post of Instructor, and drilled the lads to their hearts' content.' The account goes on to say that the boys wished to obtain dummy rifles, as would be used by the early BB companies. The locals of Thurso used to joke that they were the home of the first BB company, not Glasgow!

William's mother, Harriet Fraser (1833–1895), was an altogether different influence on his life. Although very little is recorded about her, her obituary states that she was 'a lady of very loving and gentle nature, sanctified by the Spirit in whom the grace of God worked mightily'. The same source goes on to describe her as 'very successful with young children in Sabbath School work; a class of thirty would be gathered about her, all attached to her with strong affection'. When considering his parents' influence, it is tempting to point out that their separate interests encapsulate the inspiration for the early Boys' Brigade movement.

The founder with the 1st Thurso Company in around 1910. (Courtesy of 1st Thurso BB)

The connection to Glasgow also came from his mother: William's father David died in China in 1868, and that seems to have been the trigger for the founder's move south. The 1871 census shows William living at 28 St James Street, Govan, with his uncle Alexander Fraser and four unmarried aunts. He had entered his uncle's business, Alex Fraser & Co., in October 1869 at the age of fifteen. They were wholesale dealers of 'soft goods', principally selling shawls. This would serve as an apprenticeship for William, who continued with his uncle's business into the 1870s.

It was in the 1870s that William Smith moulded his life, and attached himself to the principles that would stick with him for the remainder of it. He became more involved in the church, joining the YMCA at the age of eighteen in 1872 and becoming a full church member on 12 April 1874, in his twentieth year. He joined the Free College Church, much to his uncle's approval. In other matters, his uncle was not so happy, for in the 1870s his late father's interests shone through as William became involved in the Volunteer movement.

The Volunteer Force was a citizen army of part-time soldiers, which was re-established in 1859 principally as a defence force for Britain. It was not a new idea, the new force being set up using the same legislation enacted to establish the force set up in 1804 to repel any Napoleonic invasion, but the fear in the 1850s was not necessarily of foreign invasion. The new force was seen as being more effective as an army reserve, and one for dealing with political unrest. The successor to the Volunteer Brigades was the Territorial Army.

William joined 'C' Company of the 1st Lanarkshire Volunteers in 1873, being promoted to corporal in 1874. Two years later he passed his lieutenant's examination, which paved his way to the officer class. According to Gibbon's history he was a popular subaltern, but 'Lieutenant Smith was a disciplinarian, a good drill and a stickler for correctness and smartness of uniform and accoutrements'. Again, this is a habit that would follow him

The founder as a young man in around 1880.

*Above*: The founder (second from left on front row) with his Volunteer unit in around 1900.

*Left*: A cap badge of the 1st Lanarkshire Rifle Volunteers unit.

through life in his leadership of the Boys' Brigade. Stress of business meant he was forced to resign his commission in 1881, but he was able to regain it two years later.

The stress that prompted him to leave the Volunteers was caused by William starting up his own independent business. Smith broke with his uncle's business apparently due to the latter's lack of interest in change. Smith believed that the business should change course with the trends, but his uncle was content. Gibbon also suggests Fraser strongly disapproved of his nephew's connection to the Volunteers, and ultimately made him choose between the business or the Volunteers. The 1881 census shows William, a thirty-year-old shawl manufacturer, living with his mother and siblings in Govan.

He started the company Smith, Smith & Co. with his brother Donald at West Nile Street, Glasgow. Soon afterwards the business was expanded with the arrival of another partner in Mr Finlay, and thus Smith, Finlay & Co. started trading.

It is clear that William Smith was an extremely busy individual. By 1883 he was earning his living from his own business, which he had started from scratch, all the while retaining his commission as a lieutenant in the Volunteers, and becoming more increasingly involved with the work of the church, particularly the youth. By that year he was also engaged to Amelia Pearson Sutherland, who he affectionately referred to as 'Pearsie'. The couple married in March 1884 and went on to have two children: George Stanley Smith, born 1889, and Douglas Pearson Smith, born 1891.

Despite all this, William still felt the need to do more within the church to help the young lads who had nothing to do in the evenings, and whose attentions perhaps drifted to trouble! As one of Smith's contemporaries put it: 'He saw the multitude of boys standing aimlessly at street corners, with nothing else to do and nowhere to go in those days.' Already active in youth work with the North Woodside Mission, Smith approached the minister with a view to starting up a new weeknight organisation for boys to get them off the street, and to direct their energy to a useful cause. When he spoke of forming a 'Brigade' based on military discipline, the Free Church minister was said to be uneasy. Nonetheless, the Mission was renowned for its far-reaching community-based work, and so it was agreed to allow this well-respected Sunday school teacher to trial this new idea.

Backed by his two old friends, brothers James R. Hill and John R. Hill, William Alexander Smith set out the blueprint for his new organisation, which was to be called 'The Boys' Brigade'.

The Smith family (left to right): Amelia; Douglas; Kate (founder's sister); George Stanley; and William Alexander.

*Left*: The founder later in life.

*Below*: The North Woodside Mission, where the founder held his Sunday school and established the Boys' Brigade. (Courtesy of John Cooper)

The current plaque at North Woodside Mission, marking the founding of the BB. (Courtesy of John Cooper)

The original plaque, which was housed inside North Woodside Mission. It is now held at Glasgow Battalion HQ. (Courtesy of John Cooper)

# Chapter 2

# The Birth of a Movement

*'On the 4th October, 1883, twenty-eight boys and teachers in a Sunday school in the north-west district of Glasgow met together, and called themselves the Boys' Brigade.'*

The above quote, the words of the founder (in his pamphlet *The Story of the Boys' Brigade)* plainly illustrates the very humble beginnings of the national movement at the Free Church Mission at 329 North Woodside Road. It was established as a small venture: an idea by a Sunday school teacher as a means to improve the school's faith outreach in the area it served, with little ambition for it to spread much further. The founder was, however, clear in his vision that the fusion of religious education and military drill would be popular with boys, and would help solve the decline faced by the Sunday schools in general.

It was not his aim or intention to boost recruitment for the army, but instead to help boost membership of churches. In his own words, 'Military organisation and drill are used as a means of securing the interest of the boys, banding them together, and the promoting among them such habits as the Brigade is designed to form.' Those habits are enshrined in the Brigade's stated Object, that being: 'The Advancement of Christ's Kingdom among Boys and the promotion of habits of reverence, discipline, self-respect and all that tends towards a true Christian manliness' ('obedience' was added in 1893).

His immediate goal in establishing his Boys' Brigade was to tackle what he recognised to be the two main failures of the existing Sunday school: boys were leaving it aged about fifteen 'under the evident impression they were too big and manly for it', and that

An example of a dummy rifle as used by many of the first BB companies. The rifles were all either 'dummy' or decommissioned, meaning they were never fired. (Courtesy of Robin Bolton)

when they did leave, most were 'growing up into rough, unmanageable fellows, without much reverence for God or man'.

Smith believed that introducing military drill was the solution to both problems. He believed that boys were 'inherently fond' of soldiering and drill, and so used this aspect not only as a means of retaining the interests of the older boys, but also to change their interpretation of what it meant to be Christian. As the founder stated in 1888: 'It also seemed to us by associating Christianity with all that was most noble and manly in a boys sight, we would be going a long way to disabuse his mind of the idea that there is anything effeminate or weak about Christianity.' Thus, it is clear that from the earliest point of its inception, the Boys' Brigade has been a vessel primarily for the church.

The motto of the Boys' Brigade was chosen as 'Sure and Stedfast', and the emblem of the organisation was the anchor. It refers to a particular verse in the bible, Hebrews 6:19: 'We have this as a sure and steadfast anchor of the soul, a hope that enters into the inner place behind the curtain.' Why the anchor was chosen is unknown. Brigade historian Robin Bolton suggests it was taken from The Foundry Boys Religious Society. Other commentators have suggested it was linked to the Smith family crest, although this was dismissed by the founder's son, Stanley.

The logo of the Boys' Brigade until 1926, featuring the plain anchor.

Being a keen Volunteer, the founder did not shy away from strict militarism. So strict was the deportment of drill that it is commonly reported that many of the very first boys left the company, finding it to be too intense! Happily, however, numbers were made up again due to popular appeal. The founder wrote that, 'Boys must come on parade looking smart and clean. The company must 'fall-in' sharp to the minute; and after being formed up in line heads are uncovered, and prayer offered.' After the opening service, 'regular military drill goes on for about three-quarters of an hour', before closing with a hymn.

A uniform was gradually introduced, but by 1885 the 1st Glasgow Company had not as yet got beyond civilian dress with 'rosettes'. From 1885 they wore a neat blue forage cap and a brown waist belt and white haversack. The *Glasgow Evening Post* stated: 'For the purpose of drill in the manual exercises they carried imitation rifles of the short Snider size.' In 1888 Smith referred to the uniform as 'of a very simple and inexpensive nature, but...neat and effective'. The uniform accoutrements are now, of course, an integral part of the historic BB identity. The role of dummy rifles in that Christian organisation would, however, eventually prove controversial to many.

The first display and inspection of Smith's 1st Glasgow Company was conducted on 19 March 1885 by Captain David Gray of the 1st Lanark Rifle Volunteers (Smith's unit). On parade were three officers and fifty-two boys (including a flute band of sixteen). In his official report Captain Gray told how in an hour and a half, 'Mr Smith put the company through seventeen different military movements in company drill, all of which were performed with a remarkable steadiness and precision.' The display was reported in most Glasgow papers, as was Captain Gray's full report, which focused mainly on the military discipline. There was no mention of the Christian outreach in any of the reports. Captain Gray finished by commenting that he trusted 'it [the BB] may spread among the community, so that others may also derive similar benefits'.

Indeed, by the time of that first inspection the 1st Glasgow were not alone, with other BB companies being formed along Smith's blueprint. In January 1885 Smith's company and that of his friend, J. B. Couper, were given the official designation of

The first known picture of the 1st Glasgow Company at Garscube House in 1885. (The Glasgow Battalion BB)

The 1st Glasgow Company in uniform at Garscube in 1885. (The Glasgow Battalion BB)

the 1st and 2nd Glasgow companies respectively. At the end of March 1885 the 3rd, 4th, 5th and 6th Glasgow companies, as well as the 1st Edinburgh were formed. Then, in October 1885, the Glasgow Battalion was formed, which then consisted of seven companies, nineteen officers and 241 NCOs and boys. The founder was appointed as the President of Glasgow Battalion, and would hold the post for five years.

Growth continued through the battalion's first session as word of the organisation spread: by April 1886 it contained twenty-five companies, seventy-eight officers, and 1,073 NCOs and boys. It is interesting to note that seventy-two of those officers were serving or past members of the Volunteers, which gives a great insight into how that movement embraced the Brigade almost as a junior branch. Boys too were keen to join, with one article in the *Glasgow Evening Express* (November 1885) advising: 'Two young correspondents wish to know where they can join the Boys' Brigade of Rifle Volunteers. If they apply to Mr Smith, of Messrs Smith, Finlay & Co., 22 West Nile Street, he will doubtless satisfy their youthful enthusiasm.'

As noted, by March 1885 the organisation had breached the city limits making it to Edinburgh. By December 1885 there were four companies in Edinburgh, and at least one company each in Manchester, Penzance, Armitage and London. The pace at which the organisation spread was remarkable. After five years the founder reported that 230 companies had been set up, composed of 800 officers and 11,000 boys. It is clear that the founder's vision had been vindicated. His idea to introduce military drill proved to be very attractive to boys aged between twelve and seventeen, and their participation in that activity with the Boys' Brigade encouraged them to have greater interaction with religion, not only on meeting nights, but also with expected attendance at Sunday school (although regrettably this aspect was largely ignored in the press reports).

The founder continued to expand the scope of activities for the Brigade, which, as we have seen, seemed to be limited to a lengthy drill parade sandwiched between two short religious services. As the 1885–86 session began, the founder encouraged members of

The 4th Glasgow Company brandishing their dummy rifles in 1888. (Courtesy of John Cooper)

First review of the Glasgow Battalion, 1886. (The Glasgow Battalion BB)

1st Glasgow Company with rifles. The founder is on the right, at the back.

One of the oldest surviving BB Colours today, the 6th London Company was formed in 1887. (Courtesy of Borneo Stedfast Heritage Project)

**THE BOYS' BRIGADE**

MEMBERSHIP CARD

SESSION   ☐   FOUNDED
1927-28        1883

PATRON H.M. THE KING

*Left*: The founder's idea of introducing camping as an activity was a masterstroke. By the turn of the century, camping was an integral part of the BB experience for boys in the summer months.

*Below*: Member of the 1st Glasgow at Tighnabruaich, the site of the first camp of 1886.

the 1st Glasgow to set aside savings which would go towards a camp. The cost was set at 9 shillings per boy. On 16 July 1886, fifty members of Smith's company, along with Smith and the Hill brothers, set off for camp at Tighnabruiach in the Kyles of Bute. Thus, the founder can also boast of being one of the pioneers of 'camping', albeit in a church hall, long before the establishment of the Boy Scouts.

The camp would, however, be no informal affair, as reported in the *Glasgow Evening Post*: 'The detachment looked very smart as they marched down to the steamer, headed by their band…and the baggage wagon laden with serviceable-looking kit bags.' Although a regatta and 'other entertainments' were organised, it was noted that 'the boys will be kept thoroughly to discipline and order during their stay'. This first camp would not be under canvas; rather, the boys and officers for this first week-long camp would be hosted at Auchlenlochan Public Hall. Summer camps would become a popular feature for many companies – or at least those that could afford it. From 1888 the 9th and 32nd Glasgow companies camped at Strachur annually until 1902, while the Glasgow Battalion organised their first Battalion Camp in 1893.

By 1890 the appeal of the Boys' Brigade had grown to the extent that the founder was compelled to resign his post as president of Glasgow Battalion. This was in order to allow more time for him to take up his duties as Brigade Secretary, which was now his full-time occupation. The Brigade had become a national organisation, and the founder would spend the rest of his life working to ensure the expansion and improvement of his Brigade around the world.

9th and 32nd Glasgow on a steamer on the way to camp at Strachur in 1892. (Courtesy of John Cooper)

9th and 32nd Glasgow boys in Sunday best in 1892: boys would still be expected to attend church while at camp. (Courtesy of John Cooper)

32nd Glasgow Company undertaking rifle practice at camp in 1892. (Courtesy of John Cooper)

*Above*: The Brigade Secretary's office in around 1900.

*Right*: The first proficiency badge for boys to wear on uniform was introduced in 1890. This badge was awarded for good conduct and good attendance.

# Imitation and Criticism

One of the strengths of Smith's Boys' Brigade was that it was non-denominational – all Christian churches were able to establish a BB company. Despite this, variations of the organisation were founded largely on the model of the BB, while remaining separate. In Scotland these were sometimes referred to as the 'Fancy Brigades'. Due to the success of the Boys' Brigade, the denominational Church Lads Brigade was formed in 1891 for boys in the Church of England. Similarly, a Jewish Lads Brigade was set up in 1895 in London by Colonel Albert E. W. Goldsmid in order to help poor immigrant Jewish boys integrate. A Catholic Boys Brigade was also set up in 1896.

In 1899, the Boys' Life Brigade (BLB) was formed. This organisation was almost identical to the Boys' Brigade, except it was founded on the principle of pacifism. Its founders were strongly against the military aspects of the BB, particularly the widespread use of dummy rifles through the organisation. The BLB were not alone in their criticism of the BB for their apparent militarism as many viewed it as training young Christian boys to become soldiers. This was a concern shared by many ministers and clergy around the country who remained uncomfortable about bringing the organisation into. their church, and it did some damage to the progress of the Brigade in its first decades.

One of the more successful youth movements to follow the lead of the Boys' Brigade was the Boy Scouts, formed in 1907. Founded by Robert Baden-Powell, it is largely forgotten just how much he was influenced by Smith and the Boys' Brigade. Prior to the establishment of the Boy Scouts, Baden-Powell was appointed an Honorary Vice-President of the Brigade in 1903, and largely came up with the Scouting programme when Smith challenged him to set out his own vision for the Brigade. At the famous experimental first Scout camp at Brownsea Island, half of the twenty participants were from public schools while the other half were taken from BB companies. It was not intended for Scouting to be a separate movement; instead, it was to be an element or activity to be introduced into other organisations. A special BB Scout uniform and scout badge to be worn in BB uniform was introduced in 1909 for those BB companies that took part in Scouting activities.

The forage cap was the first item of headwear issued to boys in 1883, and remained part of the uniform until it was ultimately phased out in 1970.

The founder with the 1st Glasgow Company Band in 1893. As with military regiments, company bands were an important activity to improve the status of companies.

The 1st Glasgow Company in the upper halls of the North Woodside Mission in 1902, where they were founded. (The Glasgow Battalion BB)

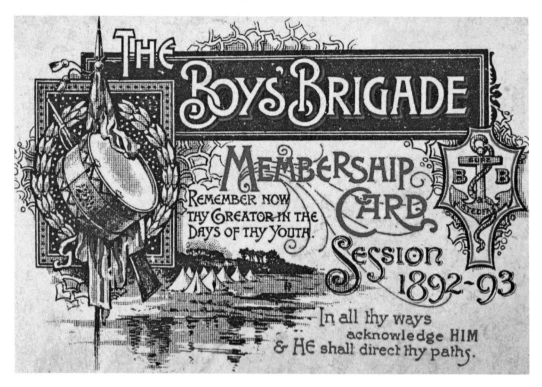

BB Membership card, 1892–93.

The founder attends a Scouting event with his friend Sir Robert Baden-Powell, the founder of the Boy Scouts.

A BB Scouting uniform was introduced in 1909 for those companies who wished to undertake Scouting activities.

A BB Scouting Badge was introduced in 1909 for companies who undertook the Scouting programme.

# Chapter 3

# The Development of Battalions

The initial success of the Boys' Brigade, with its rapid spread around Britain and the Empire, is clear, but it was not without its challenges. In many cases companies existed in isolation and suffered as an effect of lack of public appreciation, funding and activities. The chief agent in overcoming these factors was the establishment of battalions – an organised group of companies in a given area. The work of the early battalions was undoubtedly important in helping to make an often little-heard-of organisation, often viewed with suspicion, into a popular and socially acceptable one. This chapter will use the Aberdeen Battalion as a case study to demonstrate how the work of the battalion changed the city's BB from a struggling entity into the second largest battalion in Scotland within fifteen years.

The BB arrived in Aberdeen in autumn 1886 with the Ferryhill Free Church looking to expand its 'missionary' work in the city. The then Secretary of the Mission School, John M. Moir, had viewed the BB as being the best vehicle for bringing the church to the youth. This first company of 1886 consisted of two officers and eighteen boys. By the close of the session the 2nd Company was established under the captaincy of John Whytnie. There remained little support for the organisation at that time, with a lack of funds being a particular issue with regards uniform: 'The boys mustered with their forage caps (which is the only part of uniform yet served out to them)' [May 1887].

The Brigade Constitution stated that for an area to form a battalion, at least six companies must be established in the area. In Aberdeen this was achieved by 1891, and so on 20 October 1891 a meeting was held 'by general desire of the officers connected within the various companies in Aberdeen' to seek permission for the formation of the battalion. Captain Whyntie was appointed President, and the battalion was sanctioned by the Brigade Executive. As one correspondent later noted, 'In those early days the methods of the Boys' Brigade were not regarded with too kindly an eye by some of the churches, but in face of difficulties Whyntie's patient and tactful leadership firmly established the battalion.'

The main function of the battalion was to look after the interests of, and expand, the Brigade in a given area. As such, the Aberdeen Battalion set up three committees to oversee BB work among national lines. There was, of course, a Bible Class committee underlying the organisation's commitment to the church. It was key that the BB promoted its merits as a Christian organisation rather than a military one to win over

*Above*: 1st Aberdeen BB Company in 1890.

*Right*: Like the founder, John Moir was involved in Mission work when he started the 1st Aberdeen Company.

*Left*: Captain John Whyntie, President of Aberdeen Battalion (1891–1900).

*Below*: Aberdeen Battalion bearer party, 1914. (Courtesy of Aberdeen & District Battalion)

the ministers. Although ministers remained suspicious, it was a great vehicle for the church. As one Aberdeen BB captain reported in 1894: 'This company [7th Aberdeen] is recruited with boys who, with one or two exceptions, would probably be brought under no Christian influences whatsoever.'

Another important element of BB work in the 1890s was what we now call 'first aid', and an 'Ambulance' Committee was established to organise ambulance classes. It should be noted that the Ambulance Badge was the first official 'proficiency' badge issued by the BB. Started in two Glasgow BB companies, it was adopted by the battalion and became national in 1893. The last committee was drill and recreation. These committees ensured the battalion provided the boys with the basic classes they required. Battalions were also responsible for the recruitment and approval of new companies and officers, taking the strain from the Brigade Secretary.

A key aim of all battalions was to publicise the work of the BB, and to win over public support and trust in these early days. In Aberdeen a public meeting was held in 1892 to showcase the works, with activities including 'Demonstrations in Ambulance Drill, Musical Drill, and Gymnastics'. It is perhaps notable that there is no mention of rifle exercises. Due to the objection of one company in 1891, the battalion did not adopt dummy rifles, with gymnastics being the popular activity in Aberdeen. This was

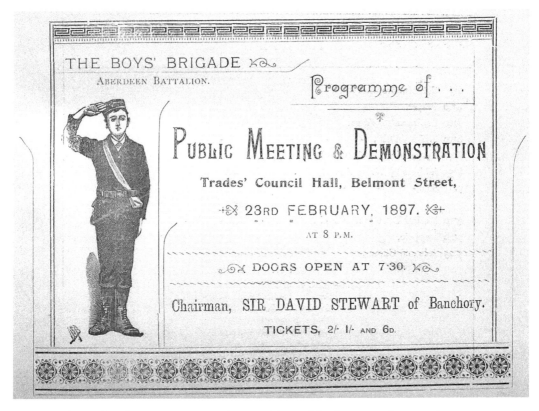

Battalions played an important part in organising public demonstrations to raise awareness of the work of the Brigade. (Courtesy of Aberdeen & District Battalion)

a tradition set by the 1st Aberdeen Coy, which stuck. The meeting was attended by the founder, but although well attended, it was a great financial loss to the battalion. A more successful public demonstration came in the next year, which 'did much to increase the interest of the general public in the work of the Brigade'. Attitudes were changing, with one battalion report stating 'the hesitation and suspicion with which many viewed [the BB] are decreasing'.

Battalions, like companies, regularly held large parades to show their strength and, as a result, promoted the learning of music. Bands were an important status symbol for battalions, which were also quite useful for drawing attention to parades. Although flute bands were more popular in the early years, Aberdeen Battalion opted to fund the development of a bugle band in 1899. Pipe bands were also popular alternatives in Scotland.

Another element of the battalion that helped expand and popularise the BB was the introduction of competition. Battalions made it possible for boys to compete for their companies rather than just for themselves. The first battalion award came in 1893 when a silver medal was awarded for ambulance class results. In 1900 the Battalion Flag was presented to the company which won the highest marks in the drill competition. The most coveted prize in Aberdeen was the Swapp Shield. This was donated to the battalion in 1897 for 'further promoting physical training among boys' in gymnastics, barbell work, Indian clubs and free movements. The Battalion Executive, wearing its PR hat, advertised these competitions and allowed the public to buy tickets

The first gymnastic team of the 1st Aberdeen Company, 1892.

Aberdeen Battalion Band in around 1900. (Courtesy of Aberdeen & District Battalion)

1st Fraserburgh BB Pipe Band in around 1924. Note the pipers' special bonnets.

to watch as spectators. The event was an annual success both with companies vying to take this most prestigious of shields, and with sell-out crowds attending the event as a popular spectacle.

In 1900 platform invitations to the Swapp competition were sent to 'Magistrates and Town Council, ministers, superintendents of sabbath schools, and headmasters of public schools', with the aim of impressing on both civic and religious society to promote growth. The annual BB gymnastic competition for the Swapp Shield continued to be a popular event into the 1960s.

Although it was by no means an easy task (progress had been met by many setbacks), it is clear Aberdeen Battalion had changed attitudes towards the BB by 1900. When the battalion was established in 1891 there were 292 boys. By 1900 there were 558. There was, however, one last aim of the battalion: to hold an annual camp under canvas. This had first been suggested in 1894, but the young battalion could not afford it. In 1900 the first camp was held at Haddo House and was an instant success. By the end of the 1900–01 session, 949 boys were on the battalion roll.

These battalion camps gave boys the chance to escape to the country for a week and proved to be very popular. It was, however, a very disciplined affair, with uniform being essential, and drill parades and inspections being carried out. By 1916 it was estimated that up to 8,534 boys attended this activity in total, which did much to keep the BB in competition with the Scouts. It was affordable to most, a boy being able to attend for 6 shillings. The inspection was always carried out by a notable figure, normally from the military. In 1910, however, the boys at camp were inspected by the founder, now Sir William, at Abyone. As the battalion entered its second decade, Whyntie stepped back to allow the charismatic George Bennett Mitchell, a local architect, to take the presidency. The camps had been his initiative, with his own company (4th Aberdeen) enjoying them from 1898.

Aberdeen BB companies would be awarded custody of the Battalion Flag if they won the annual drill competitions. (1907)

*Right*: The Swapp Shield was the most competitive and prestigious competition in Aberdeen Battalion, remaining a popular public event into the 1960s. (Courtesy of Aberdeen & District Battalion)

*Below*: 5th Aberdeen Company, winners of the first Swapp Shield in 1898.

*Above*: 1st Aberdeen Company, winners of the Swapp Shield in 1900.

*Left*: G. Bennett Mitchell MBE, President of Aberdeen Battalion (1900–41), was a huge figure in the BB nationally.

4th Aberdeen buglers at camp, 1898. (Courtesy of Aberdeen & District Battalion)

4th Aberdeen Company at camp, 1898. (Courtesy of Aberdeen & District Battalion)

4th Aberdeen Company at camp, 1898. (Courtesy of Aberdeen & District Battalion)

The founder inspects the Aberdeen Battalion on their way to camp at Aboyne in 1910. (Courtesy of Aberdeen & District Battalion)

The founder leaving the camp at Aboyne in 1910. (Courtesy of Aberdeen & District Battalion)

The progress of the battalion meant that in September 1905, Aberdeen was chosen to host the national Brigade Council. This was a huge spectacle in the city, with additional displays for visiting guests and a BB rally comprised of home and visiting companies of 1,200 boys and officers. This had a monumental impact on the battalion, which ended the session with 2,102 members. By 1905/6, the battalion had doubled in number over a three-year period. No Aberdeen company had lapsed since 1902, which had been the longest period without a company falling. This strength was demonstrated the following year when 1,850 boys and officers were on parade for the king and queen's visit to the city.

Although Aberdeen has been used as an example in this chapter, battalions around the country were carrying out similar work to ensure the furtherance of the Brigade. While some in society continued to view the BB as militarising youth (especially due to continued used of dummy rifles), the battalions were an important tool in publicising the true work of the BB as local agencies, which brought Christianity to the young while moulding them into useful citizens. The beauty of the battalion PR machine was that it increased the organisational capacity of the Brigade to allow local people to see for themselves what the organisation was all about. For the majority of them, this was a positive experience.

The work of battalions also helped to develop the national strategy of the Brigade as success stories were carried back to the founder at conferences, in writing and by what he witnessed on his extensive visits around the country. In the beginning, the Boys' Brigade existed for instilling military discipline and Christian faith. As time wore on, a badge scheme developed, adding more popular and useful skills for boys to learn and take part in. It is no surprise that many of the badges introduced reflected the popular activities undertaken by Aberdeen and other battalions across the nation. Proficiency badges introduced included: Ambulance (1893); Scouting (1909); Bugler (1909); Signalling (1911); Life Saving (1914); Band (1914); Physical Training/Gymnastics (1917); and the Piper badges (1921).

By 1910 the Brigade had clearly made its mark on society as an established and well-known organisation that, on the whole, was viewed as being useful to the nation. King Edward VII knighted the founder in 1909 for services to the Boys' Brigade – just another example of national acceptance. The following year, with the accession of George V, the king himself became the Patron of the Boys' Brigade. The organisational work of the Battalions did much to propel the Boys' Brigade into this position in the national consciousness.

*Above left*: The commemorative badge for the 1905 Brigade Council held at Aberdeen.

*Above right*: Aberdeen Battalion were able to build a Battalion HQ in 1909, which became the nerve centre of their activities.

*Above*: Public sports days were held annually to help further engage with the people of the city.

*Right*: The full set of badges available to boys in 1914. Second row (left to right): Life Saving Badge; Bugler's Badge; Scouting Badge; Signalling Badge. The Ambulance Badge is front and centre.

# Chapter 4

# The First World War – The Vindication of the BB?

In 1913 King George V gave permission for a King's Badge to be awarded in the Brigade. Following on from the knighthood of the founder, this demonstrated that the Boys' Brigade had made it into the national consciousness.

The badge – the highest in the Boys' Brigade – would not be an easy one to obtain. The recipient had to be no less than sixteen years of age and complete at least three BB sessions with good conduct. In addition the recipient had to have attended a minimum of at least 90 per cent of company drill classes and Sunday school classes. Bear in mind that the majority of boys of that age would normally be seeking or already be in employment – particularly in the lower classes. All this would mean that the presentation of the early badges were not so common.

The first of the King's Badges were presented in the second half of the 1913–14 session. The very first badge was presented to Colour Sergeant William Gant of the 2nd Nottingham Company on 10 February 1914. Being a special occasion, the presentation was made by Brigade President Lord Guthrie. A handful of other badges were presented in the same session, but with little note or fanfare, which may well be the reason why the records of early presentations are so poor. The badge continues to be the highest award in the Boys' Brigade, although for the majority of its existence it has been awarded as a Queen's Badge. The design of the badge has been fairly consistent though the years: the BB anchor surmounted by the royal crown. The exception to this was a barrel badge, produced in the 1960s to match a redesign of the achievement badges.

The awarding of such royal patronage in 1914 should have made it a memorable year of celebration for the Brigade. Sadly, history would relegate these first awards to nothing more than an almost forgotten footnote as double tragedy was to hit the Brigade in only a matter of months.

The first tragedy would occur with the death of Sir William Alexander Smith. He had been a tireless promoter of his Brigade until the very end, suffering a stroke on 10 May 1914 while attending a BB Executive meeting after a BB display in the Royal Albert Hall. By the time of his death, the organisation he founded with a handful of boys in a church hall in Glasgow in 1883 had grown to an organisation with 70,000 members in the United Kingdom, and with a worldwide membership of 120,000 boys.

When the founder's body arrived back in Glasgow for the funeral, 7,000 boys lined the funeral route to his final resting place. Among them was Col/Sgt Arthur J. Reid, often

*Above left*: The membership card for 1910–11. In that year, George V became the first monarch to be Patron of the Boys' Brigade. (Courtesy of Borneo Stedfast Heritage Project)

*Above right*: The King's Badge as designed in 1913.

The funeral procession of the founder.

The funeral cortège of the founder. Arthur J. Reid of the 1st Glasgow, first in Scotland to be presented with a King's Badge, is seen wearing the badge. (Courtesy of Robin Bolton)

*Above left:* Memorial plaque to the founder at St Giles Cathedral, Edinburgh.

*Above right*: The founder's final resting place at the Western Necropolis, Glasgow.

credited as the first Kingsman (and certainly the first in Scotland). Present at the founder's funeral were representatives of the Church Lads' Brigade, the Catholic Boys' Brigade, the Jewish Boys' Brigade, the Boys' Life Brigade and, of course, Sir Robert Baden-Powell of the Boy Scouts, who came to salute this pioneer to whom they all owed their respective successes.

As the founder was laid to rest in the Western Necropolis, members of the 1st Glasgow Company filed past the graveside, each member dropping a white flower into the grave of their departed captain. Little did they know that within few short months they would find themselves in the midst of even greater national tragedy, which would have fatal consequences for many who were present that day.

# War

The outbreak of the Great War in August 1914 had an immediate impact on the work of the Boys' Brigade. The principal problem suffered was due to the Brigade's connection to its most enthusiastic backers before the war: associations with the Volunteers and Territorials. The smooth running of the Brigade depended on the voluntary service of thousands of trained men, who were now being called to the service of their country.

The exodus of BB officers for war service left many companies struggling to provide their normal programme for the boys still attending weekly drill meetings. This was something that was further exacerbated in 1916 with the introduction of conscription. The Brigade had very few options available to better the situation, and became more reliant on the older officers who escaped war duties and the senior boys who were able to escape munitions work.

So serious was the concern that at the Brigade Council in 1916, G. Bennett Mitchell, President of Aberdeen Battalion, ran a seminar on 'How can we carry on during the War?': 'He referred to the shortage of officers, and said the only way to overcome it was for every officer who remained to make up his mind to harder work and greater effort than he had ever put before.' The work of the Brigade would change during the war due to necessity, but this change was cleverly disguised as a means of being seen to be useful to the war effort.

After only one year of war, the Brigade was keen to point out how useful it had been as an organisation in aiding the war effort. At the Brigade Council of 1915, Brigade President Lord Guthrie highlighted the 'vast amounts of work of various kinds' that had been carried out by the boys and their companies. The boys were volunteering in hospitals and undertaking other useful works, but perhaps the greatest asset they had was the organisational and logistical potential of the strong battalions they had helped to raise by 1914.

These highly organised units allowed them to gather huge amounts of funds for good causes. Guthrie explained: 'They had been instrumental in collecting many thousands of pounds for the Red Cross … and had raised £3,000 for equipping and maintaining recreational huts for the soldiers in France.' This new focus for the Brigade during the war years gave it greater popular purpose, and initially led to an increase in membership while officer numbers dropped. In order to recognise the good work of their members a National Service badge was introduced in 1915 for boys who completed 100 hours of voluntary work benefitting the war effort.

*Above left*: Lord Guthrie, a Scottish judge and lawyer, served as President of the Boys' Brigade from 1910 to 1919.

*Above right*: During the war, the Aberdeen Battalion HQ was taken over and used as a central depot for the British Red Cross. (Courtesy of Aberdeen & District Battalion)

A rest hut for servicemen that was built with money raised by the Edinburgh Battalion.

The Brigade Council went a step further in 1918 when it voted to allow companies to enrol themselves as Cadet Units. The BB Cadets were given national funding from the War Office on the understanding that they taught certain military procedures. This included being formed into cadet battalions and also led to the introduction of a BB Cadet uniform, which was markedly more militaristic than the standard BB uniform. The Council only agreed to set up these units because they believed it would not interfere with the religious or moral work the Brigade was carrying out.

The Brigade had another record to boast about during the war, and it was a record which they proudly used to discredit their most vocal pre-war critics. Some elements of pre-war society lambasted the BB for its militaristic nature and disagreed profusely with the training of boys in any military discipline – however soft. After thirty years of training boys, there were now hundreds of thousands of BB trained boys-come-men serving the nation.

They were quick to sign up. Many answered Kitchener's call to serve 'King and Country' and joined as members of the so-called 'pals battalions'. As early as September 1914, G. A. Oliver, former Captain of the 1st Hull Company, reported that: 'I find that a large number of them [Old Boys] are already enrolled. I heard of one party of seventeen young fellow members of the brotherhood, and mainly Old Boys of the 1st Hull Company, who volunteered as a body.' Perhaps the most well-known example of such camaraderie was in the formation of the 16th Battalion Highland Light Infantry.

The 16th Battalion was formed in Glasgow in September 1914 with such a high concentration of BB Old Boys that it was often given the suffix the 'Boys' Brigade Battalion'. There were three Glasgow City volunteer battalions: the first from the tramways employees (The 15th HLI – known as 'The Boozy 1st'), the Boys' Brigade (The 16th HLI – known as the 'Holy 2nd') and the Chamber of Commerce (The 17th HLI – known as the 'Featherbeds'). Consequence would have it that the battalion

The BB National Service Badge was awarded to boys who aided the war effort.

*Above*: The 2nd Dorchester BB Cadet unit in their uniforms at camp. (Courtesy of the family of W. C. Marshallsay)

*Left*: A BB Cadet cap badge. (Courtesy of the family of W. C. Marshallsay)

*Above*: The 16th Battalion Highland Light Infantry parading under their BB colour in 1914. The inspection was carried out by the Lord Provost of Glasgow.

*Right*: When the national call for volunteers came in September 1914, the Boys' Brigade were commended for the high number of trained Old Boys who signed up, many in pals battalions.

fell under the command of Colonel David Laidlaw, who had been involved with the Boys' Brigade since 1885 and served as Treasurer of Glasgow Battalion and a Brigade Vice-President.

This huge response from thousands of Old Boys and officers even drew comment from King George V, who congratulated the Brigade 'on the vast numbers of past members who are now serving at the front'. There were many estimates as to how many actually served. In September 1918, as the war was drawing to a close, Lord Guthrie estimated that as many as 800,000 men and boys with associations to the BB had 'done their bit'. When the war had ended, a more precise evaluation revised that number to about 400,000 on active service. The BB Battle Honours too were well publicised, with ten Victoria Crosses, nineteen Distinguished Service Orders, seventy-three Distinguished Conduct Medals, seventy-nine Military Crosses and 139 Military Medals being awarded to Old Boys and officers. Inevitably there was a great loss of life, with Boys' Brigade Rolls of Honour commemorating more than 50,000 Old Boys who were killed in the conflict.

The Aberdeen Battalion War Memorial carries the names of 304 Old Boys and officers who were killed during the First World War. (Courtesy of Aberdeen & District Battalion)

Among the dead were Frank E. Smith (1st Warley), who was killed in November 1916 aged nineteen, and Drummer Thomas Cruickshank (18th Aberdeen), who was also killed in 1916 aged nineteen. The former was one of the first to be awarded the King's Badge in 1914, and the latter was the first to gain the same award in Aberdeen Battalion. Perhaps they, more than most, represent the lost promise that 1914 delivered to the Brigade.

The same fate befell many of those who had signed up with the 16th Battalion Highland Light Infantry, which was all but annihilated during the Battle of the Somme in November 1916. At Beaumont-Hamel, of the twenty-one officers and 650 who originally enlisted with the unit, only thirteen officers and 390 men survived.

Although the Brigade emerged from the war as strong as it had been, many companies did not. In Fraserburgh, for example, all six of the regular officers who staffed the 1st Fraserburgh found themselves on war duties of one description or another, which led to the company being placed in abeyance for the war years. During the conflict, three of the officers were killed, and therefore the company was not resurrected when the survivors returned. This was the scenario suffered by many companies the length of the country.

As the organisation emerged from war, it would actively seek to distance itself from the accusations of its militarism of youth that had plagued it since its creation in 1883.

A Boys' Brigade recruiting scene in around 1920.

# Chapter 5

# Post-War Expansion and Union

For many the First World War was greeted as the 'vindication' of the Boys' Brigade. The organisation had proven its worth to its critics, and was seen to do its bit for King and Country. The Brigade had a very slight boost as now an organisation offering soft militarism was nothing to be ashamed of in a highly militarised nation.

The first part of recovery would be in restarting companies in the areas where they had disappeared during the war. These were being re-established promptly, in many cases with new men being required to replace the fallen. This was the case in Fraserburgh in 1921 when a new company was formed in place of the old. All of the officers of that new company had served in and received their training during the First World War. The impetus for that company came from the Revd W. Neil Sutherland – a man of God who served as a major during the war and emerged decorated with a Military Cross. Significantly, this new company did not bear the dummy rifles of the old Fraserburgh Company as the Revd Sutherland wanted a Brigade in order to rebuild his Sunday school.

The organisation would further expand with the introduction of a new junior section, which had its beginnings in 1917 – the Boy Reserves. It emerged from a national conference to deal with the significant decrease of younger boys attending Sunday school during the war years. Convened by the Archbishop of Canterbury, and supported by representatives from across all groups and societies, the BB was represented by Carey Longmore (Captain, 1st Warley Company). The Archbishop had pointed out how serious this decline in Sunday school attendance would be for the BB of the future, which drew its young membership from the churches. A new organisation for younger boys would be required, which would make Sunday school attendance compulsory.

This had not been the first call for younger boys to be brought under the umbrella of the Brigade. There had been a number of calls for the joining age to be reduced from twelve, but it was largely ignored. Instead, a sizable number of companies simply admitted younger boys against the rules stated in the constitution, or simply set up their own independent junior sections connected to churches. Aside from Longmore, Plymouth Battalion had made an application for a junior corps to be established in January 1917.

Longmore brought his own proposal to the Executive with a vision of this junior corps, which would be constituted as a separate organisation for boys aged nine to eleven. A committee was set up by the Executive to explore this 'experimental' organisation. It would, of course, need a name. Many were considered including the 'Busy Bees' (BBs), but in the end Longmore's suggestion of the 'Boy Reserves' was adopted. Bennett Mitchell of Aberdeen Battalion was on the committee that helped develop the organisation, and recalled one meeting beginning at 9 a.m. and stretching to 11 p.m.!

*Above*: A Boy Reserves Team in Aberdeen in around 1923. (Courtesy of Aberdeen & District Battalion)

*Right*: A leader's cap badge showing the logo of the Boy Reserves.

The Brigade Executive approved of the introduction of the Boy Reserves at Brigade Council at Manchester in September 1917. The approved activities of this new organisation could not have been overly appealing: 'The first Boy Reserves manual listed thirty different drill movements but only ten different games – and the only other recommended activity was knot tying.' Considering this new organisation was aimed at boys aged from between nine to eleven, it is little surprise that the activities quickly diversified to shun the drill movements in favour of more games.

It must be admitted that this new organisation was not initially popular, and given the strength of the senior organisation, was slow to roll out. In 1918, in its second year, there were only fifty-nine Boy Reserves teams in the UK compared to 1,078 companies. By 1920 the number of teams had only increased to 209.

It is perhaps worthy at this point, considering the gender balance of BB officers today, to mention that the introduction of the Boy Reserves led to the appointments of the first female leaders associated with the BB in 1919. Although it would be decades before they were accorded equal rank, women were allowed to serve in these sections as 'Brigade Instructors'. The most famous of these instructors was Miss Dora Webb, who toured the country promoting the Boy Reserves and, later, the Life Boys.

Further expansion of the organisation still preoccupied the minds of the Brigade Executive. By the 1920s there was a glaring awareness that the organisation, despite its apparent vindication, was still suffering from its image as an extension of state militarism. In the height of the war, state-sponsored BB Cadet units had been set up 'without in any way affecting the religious or social side of the work'. In 1924 the rules were changed, with the authorities insisting these sponsored units 'required affiliation to an army unit, and laid down that the training must conform to syllabus prescribed by the military authorities'.

The Executive rejected these new terms, and put an end to the BB Cadet units, finding them to be 'contrary to the wishes of churches, detrimental to the extension of the Brigade, and opposed to its highest interests'. This put to an end the most controversial companies in the history of the BB and it was widely welcomed. Captain Charles Fraser, President of Inverness Battalion, said of the cadet scheme: 'It was a source of perpetual annoyance as long as we [the BB] were in it, and now churches were whole-heartedly with us!'

Now that the Cadet Units had been consigned to history, the Brigade Council of 1924 turned its attention to a more longstanding militaristic tradition of the Brigade: the use of model or deactivated rifles in drill. A report from the Executive recorded 'a growing feeling throughout the Brigade in favour of discarding the model rifle altogether'. Like with the Cadet Units, they viewed it as 'detrimental to the extension of the Brigade'. Figures obtained by the Executive showed that in 1924 only 405 companies – or 30 per cent – still used model rifles, but Stanley Smith, son of the founder, made the argument that even this minority was tainting the reputation of the Brigade: 'Even in districts where the rifle was not actually in use, the mere fact that it was sanctioned was sufficient for its retention to do incalculable harm to the development and extension of the movement'.

The issue was put to a referendum of all companies in 1925: 917 votes in favour of discontinuing rifles, 228 against discontinuing, with 230 not voting. In other words two thirds approved of the removal of rifles. With that result, the Executive and Council

*Copy! original sent to Glasgow 4/4/24.*

**B.R. 17.**

# THE BOY RESERVES.

THE TRAINING RESERVE OF THE BOYS' BRIGADE.

OBJECT.—The advancement of Christ's Kingdom among young Boys, and the training of a body of suitable Recruits for The Boys' Brigade.

4th Aberdeen SECTION.

### DECLARATION BY PROPOSED HONORARY INSTRUCTOR.

I, Florence A. Mackay having studied the Constitution and Regulations of The Boy Reserves, desire to be enrolled as an HONORARY INSTRUCTOR in the 4th Aberdeen Section of The Boy Reserves, and I am in complete sympathy with the object of the Organization.

Signature, Florence A. Mackay

To be Countersigned by the Captain of the Section, } Signature, H. G. Williams

John D. Ledingham

Date, 5th March 1924.

*Above*: Honorary Instructors signed declarations to acknowledge they were in sympathy to the aims of the organisation. (Courtesy of Aberdeen & District Battalion)

*Right*: Donald Finnemore's design for the new BB logo.

decreed that no BB company would be permitted to use model rifles after 31 May 1926. The rifle would not be a big miss, as the *Dundee Courier* reported: 'The Boy Scouts seem to get on with no more lethal weapon than a simple pole, so the BB should not greatly miss their model rifles.' Bennett Mitchell boasted that Aberdeen Battalion had never used them and they had not suffered for it: 'From an Aberdonian point of view, why should we pay for rifles when we could do without them?'

The wording of all the Executive's statements regarding expansion makes clear that all these moves had been planned. The expansion they spoke of had been a desired amalgamation with the Boys' Life Brigade (BLB) – an organisation that mirrored the activities of the BB, but utterly detested and opposed the mix of militarism and Christianity in the youth. Attempts at amalgamation had been made in 1914, and again in 1920 when talks broke down over the BB involvement in the cadet scheme and the use of model rifles. Both of these problematic issues were now gone.

After over a year of negotiations between the BB and the BLB, the Brigade Council approved the amalgamation in September 1926 with only very minor opposition. The BLB followed suit the following month, the argument for union being passionately articulated by D. L. Finnemore, from Birmingham, who made a 'convincing argument of the benefit which the work among boys will derive from the fusion of the two organisations'. In final negotiations all use of the word military was removed from the constitution in order to placate the partnership, which in some way went against the original vision of the founder.

Nearly fifty years after the Brigade's formation by Smith, the amalgamation was clearly required. In 1925 the Boys' Brigade had a membership of 60,000 boys in the UK, with an additional 19,000 in the Boy Reserves. In comparison, the Boys' Life Brigade enjoyed a membership of 21,000 with their junior section, The Lifeboys, comprising 8,500 boys. It must be noted that, as with much of the 'Fancy Brigades', the majority of their membership was in England and Wales – particularly in the English cities. Thus, when amalgamation was completed, the number of Boys' Brigade members

An example of a pre-1927 plain anchor on an officer's cap badge and collar badges.

in England and Wales jumped from 27,000 to 45,000, while there was little impact on Scottish numbers.

While the BLB was happy to fall under the name of the Boys' Brigade, symbolic changes were made in order to acknowledge their separate pasts. A new logo would need to be designed for all uniforms, which would be introduced immediately. A number of designs were drawn up to symbolise the marriage of the two organisations by incorporating the anchor of the Boys' Brigade with the red cross of the BLB. Donald Finnemore himself drew up some suggestions, but the new design would be simple: a central anchor with a red cross behind it. While this was a symbolic adaption, real change would be required to make the marriage work.

The logo of the Boys' Life Brigade was dominated by a red cross, which was incorporated into the new Boys' Brigade logo in 1926. (Courtesy of Borneo Stedfast Heritage Project)

The logo as updated in 1926 to include the cross of the Boys' Life Brigade. As demonstrated here, all badges and uniform had to be updated to reflect the change.

# Chapter 6

# For Kings and Country

Changes in symbolism and logos was one thing, but for this new union to work it would require changes to the programme of the Brigade too. These changes are perhaps best demonstrated by the expansion of the badge system, which grew to take in new skills and interests. Although most activities were already part of the BB programme, between 1926 and 1946 the Camping Badge, Arts and Crafts Badge, Swimming Badge, Firefighting Badge, Citizenship Badge and the Wayfarer Badge were introduced. The union therefore not only increased membership, but also increased the skills that would now be taught and learned through Boys' Brigade work. With the exception of drill and rank, most references to militarism were removed; the BB would now produce useful citizens. There were also many changes in uniform with the introduction of a 'field-service' cap as a regular uniform cap as well as the BLB field-Service cap being integrated with the

The post-1926 BB badges. The bottom row of six badges were all introduced as a result of the amalgamation. (Courtesy of Borneo Stedfast Heritage Project)

uniform, known as the 'B' and 'C' uniforms. This did not replace the pillbox hat outright, but served as an alternative and provided for former BLB companies who had ditched the forage cap in 1918. The BLB Sgts uniform red sash was also introduced along with a special field-service Sgts cap. Companies wearing the B or C uniforms would wear black belts rather than brown ones. The concept of a 'full-uniform' for former BLB companies was retained. A new rank of Warrant-Officer was also introduced with its own special badges.

The Boy Reserves also went through change as they were rebranded with the name of the BLB's junior reserve, but now spelt with three words: The Life Boys. Like the BR, a Life Boy team would operate separately from the BB company but would be connected to a church, and so promote its members to parent BB companies. It maintained a programme of 'physical activities, games, singing, musical marching, handicrafts, hobbies and nature study'. Punctuality remained strict, as did the requirement to attend church and Sunday school weekly. The uniform remained similar to the Boy Reserves', consisting of a navy blue (and famously itchy) polo neck jumper with the Life Boy badge on the left breast, navy blue knee-length socks and the equally famous sailor hat. The 'school cap' worn by the BLB Lifeboys was also retained as an alternative headgear. Although negotiations for union had been hard work, the amalgamation went extraordinarily smoothly, with the following decade being one of great celebration for the Brigade.

The largest of these celebrations came in 1932–33 as the Brigade marked its fiftieth anniversary. This golden jubilee was celebrated the length and breadth of the country, as well as in the countless overseas territories where the Brigade was flourishing. The greatest celebrations, of course, took place in Glasgow where it all began. The climax to the international celebrations was held in September 1933, where over 30,000 boys and officers gathered at Queen's Park for a jubilee parade. Boys from seventeen battalions took part, including representatives from the United Kingdom, China, Africa, India, Denmark and Latvia, proving the international reach of the organisation.

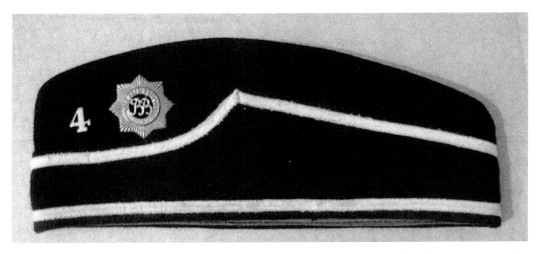

The field service cap was introduced as an alternative to the longstanding forage cap, again due to the amalgamation with the BLB.

Pictured in 1954 are, from left to right, the sons of the founder, Douglas P. Smith and G. Stanley Smith, and Donald Finnemore. Stanley served as Secretary of the BB from 1925 to 1954 while Finnemore was an important proponent of the 1926 Union from the side of the Boys' Life Brigade.

Leader's cap badge (above) and boy's badge (below) depicting the logo of the Life Boys.

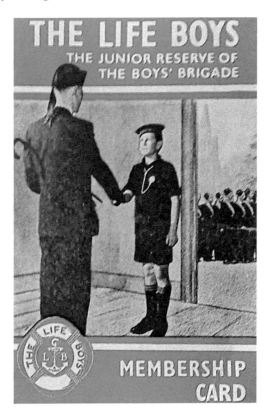

*Right*: A Life Boys membership card highlights the fact the sections function as a feed to the Boys' Brigade.

*Below*: Team games and fitness made up a large part of the Life Boy's activities.

The Duke of York was the Brigade's chief guest, representing his father, George V: 'The King wishes me to assure the officers and boys of the Brigade how pleased His Majesty is to be Patron of an institution which takes so active and public spirited a view of its duties'. The King further acknowledged the Brigade's 'valuable service to the youth of our country'. To mark the fiftieth anniversary, the Duke of York was enrolled as a member of the Boys' Brigade, the start of a connection that would last the rest of his life. The final act of commemoration came in the form of a bronze time capsule, in which the boys of 1933 wrote a message to the boys of 1983. The Jubilee Casket was then sealed for the next fifty years, until the BB centenary.

More commemorations would follow in 1935 for the Silver Jubilee of King George V. The King had served as Patron of the Boys' Brigade for thirty-eight years by the time of his jubilee, and as such the Brigade celebrated it with a national event: a baton relay. Silver batons, surmounted by a BB crest, contained a message from the Boys' Brigade to

*Left*: A commemorative Jubilee buttonhole issued to celebrate the 1933 Golden Jubilee of the Boys' Brigade. (Courtesy of Borneo Stedfast Heritage Project)

*Below*: The 1933 Jubilee Review of the Boys' Brigade in Glasgow.

The signatories of the Jubilee message representing the UK and overseas pose for a picture with the Jubilee Casket.

The 1933 Jubilee Casket.

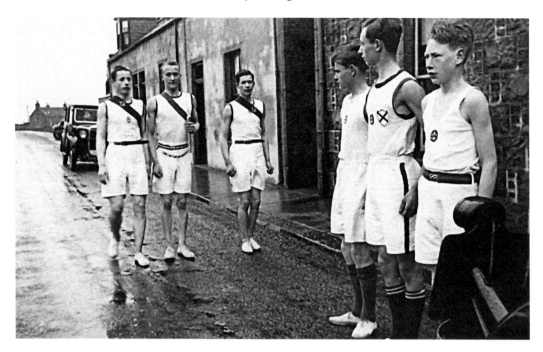

*Above*: The Silver Jubilee Baton relay of 1935 exchanges from the Fraserburgh boys to the Sandhaven boys.

*Left*: The baton used for the King's Silver Jubilee in 1935 was used again in 2012 when a similar relay was run to mark the Queen's Diamond Jubilee. (Copyright of the Boys' Brigade)

the King and were carried by a bearer and two escorts. Perhaps to emphasise the King's gift to the organisation in 1913, it was decided that where possible the bearer was to be a recipient of the King's Badge. The batons were carried the length of the country – about 2,309 miles in total – allowing as many boys as possible to take part. The message was read at every town and city it passed through, before finally being presented to the Duke of York at its conclusion.

The King died less than twelve months later, and as such the new king, Edward VIII, was invited and accepted the role in his father's place. The fact that this patronage passed

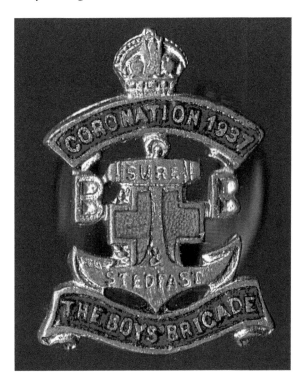

The first BB royal commemorative badge was issued in 1937 for the Coronation of the new Patron, King George VI.

with succession perhaps shows the place the organisation had taken in the national consciousness. Abdication, however, saw the quick conclusion of that appointment, and so the Duke of York, now King George VI, became Patron of the Boys' Brigade in January 1937. It was fitting for the Brigade, as the new king had shown more of an interest in the BB than King Edward ever had. The Coronation in May 1937, which fell during what was the annual display month for most companies, was used as an excuse for further celebration. The first Coronation badge was issued by the Boys' Brigade in 1937, which began a tradition marked at every Coronation and Royal Jubilee since.

# War

The celebrations of 1933, 1935 and 1937 would not be repeated in 1939 as for a second time the country, and the Boys' Brigade, was plunged into the chaos of another world war. As was noted at the time, when the First World War broke out most companies were at camp, but this time war broke out just as companies were preparing to restart. The timing could not have been worse for the Brigade, as once again officers went off to serve King and Country while, unlike last time, thousands of boys became displaced evacuees.

During this war the disruption was extended to include many bombs raining down from the skies, which often scattered BB companies in urban areas. It was recorded that by March 1941 the churches and halls of 100 companies had been bombed, while many more had been appropriated for war uses. In the same year it was recorded that 43 per cent of companies in 'severely bombed battalions' were in abeyance, the general figure being 20 per cent of companies in abeyance in England, and 8 per cent in Scotland. Figures indicate that the number of BB members fell from 92,138 in 1938 to a low of 64,747 in 1944. Life Boy members fell by 20,000 over the same period.

Something had to be done and so Brigade Secretary G. Stanley Smith headed the rallying call for companies to continue: 'Training Courses have ceased, the usual hall may not be available and our best officers may be away, but for the sake of the boys let us not be content until ways and means are found to enable us to hold our regular parade.' This generally meant the older officers and NCOs had to step up, but as with the last war the Brigade willingly altered its activities to be useful to the war effort. The pages of the *BB Gazette* were full of companies taking the initiative and lending their services to useful civil defence work.

During the first year of the war Edinburgh Battalion opened a 'Boys' Brigade Church of Scotland Canteen for Servicemen', much along the same lines as the huts funded during the First World War. Battalions and companies also did their bit to help at the home front in the civil defence movement. The boys of Birmingham Battalion served as messengers for the hospitals, while boys who received their training from the BB supported the Air Raid Precautions (ARP) wardens and Auxiliary Fire Service. This was

A wartime recruitment poster for the Boys' Brigade, as printed in 1940.

Many companies across Britain lapsed during the war due to lack of officers. Lapsing in 1940, the 1st Fraserburgh was re-established in 1944 under the leadership of NCOs and Captain Tom Ingram, a First World War veteran (seated right).

BB members taking part in fire-fighting practice during the war.

BB National Service
Badge for the Second
World War, as issued
to boys from 1940 for
undertaking 100 hours
of voluntary service.
(Courtesy of Borneo
Stedfast Heritage Project)

the form of service the Brigade preferred to support with the Executive encouraging battalions to offer Home Defence training courses. To further encourage and reward this type of service in the Brigade, the National Service Badge was issued for boys who undertook at least 100 hours of 'voluntary and unpaid national service for the community'.

Due to the union with the BLB in 1926, the BB was careful to navigate away from any military organisation such as the Cadet Force. As Mr Ron Staniford of the 1st Bletchley recorded in June 1942: 'Most companies and officers will have been disturbed by the formation in their towns of cadet units, recruiting down to the age of fourteen and drilling on Sunday mornings'! The Brigade encouraged boys to undertake some form of national service from the date of their sixteenth birthday, but it 'did not feel justified in sanctioning' affiliation to the Cadet Force. They held the view that the Cadet Force 'would not increase the effectiveness' of their training, and 'might lead to the religious aims of the Brigade being compromised'. This should be of no surprise, as any association with the cadet units would have risked a schism between the old BB and BLB contingents.

The Brigade's Diamond Jubilee was celebrated in 1943, with the war causing these celebrations to be muted. A jubilee parade was held in Windsor Castle, inspected by BB Patron King George VI. In his remarks he said: 'I feel sure that the BB will go from strength to strength, because it is built upon the twin pillars of religion and discipline and so is meeting two of the greatest needs of the present time.' These twin pillars not only preserved the BB through war, but in peacetime they propelled a great recovery in remarkably short time.

The Aberdeen Battalion War Memorial for those who fell during the Second World War bears the names of 179 officers and Old Boys. (Courtesy of Aberdeen & District Battalion)

King George VI inspects the Boys' Brigade at Windsor Castle in 1943 to mark the Diamond Jubilee of the BB.

# Chapter 7

# Golden Age and Reorganisation

The Boys' Brigade entered the 1950s with a membership of 145,000 boys (including Life Boys), proving that its ability to adapt with the times had kept it in good stead. As has been seen, the BB's offer to boys in its official programme had expanded with the badge programme, which made boys into physically fit and community-minded Christians. Not only were the new additions popular, but the old favourites of camps and PT competitions continued to appeal to the youth of the 1950s. This post-war golden age of the BB would stretch to the end of the decade before the 1960s marked the beginning of an era of struggle.

The founder's centenary celebrations in 1954 perhaps best show how the Boys' Brigade was now beginning to become set in its ways, as many of the activities planned had gone unchanged from the 1930s. It cannot be claimed the celebrations were not a success, but the three main events were a gathering of Old Boys in the Albert Hall, a torch relay from Thurso to Glasgow and an International Camp on the playing fields of Eton. The most popular and long-remembered of those events was the Founder's Camp at Eton, where boys from twenty countries were in attendance. Sir Donald Finnemore, who was an important figure in cementing BB/BLB union, was 'Camp Commandant'. The founder's centenary years also saw G. Stanley Smith, son of the founder, retire as Brigade Secretary after almost thirty years.

If the BB did have a problem in this decade, it was with the retention of older boys and the difficulty in holding onto officers after the age of eighteen. This was an issue that was exacerbated following the war, with compulsory national service for all young men aged between seventeen and twenty-one, who were required to undertake eighteen months of service. To tackle this shortage the 1954 Brigade Executive considered enhanced leadership training: 'The King George VI Foundation was giving a substantial amount towards BB training, and the Training Committee would in due course announce its proposal in this connection.' For over sixty years now the training centres at Felden Lodge and Carronvale House have been training KGVI cadets as the leaders of the future.

Another important development within the Brigade was the introduction of the Duke of Edinburgh Award in 1956. The Executive was not initially keen to participate in the award programme, believing their existing award structure to be more than adequate for the boys. Thankfully, their attitude was quick in changing and the DoE Award

*Right*: The badge for the founder's centenary camp, which was held on the playing fields at Eton.

*Below*: The King George VI cadet training scheme, which was introduced in the 1950s, continues to be run annually at Carronvale House (pictured) and Felden Lodge.

became a well-known feature in most BB companies. Initially only available to boys aged fourteen to eighteen years, this new activity, if offered, helped to separate the older boys from the younger boys, helping to retain the older boys. The activities again tended to mirror what the BB was already offering, but in many areas it enhanced and offered more specialist skills while enabling participants to gain a prestigious qualification to accompany the Queen's Badge. The DoE award continues to be a popular draw, particularly for adventure activities, to the boys of the twenty-first century.

Further change was on the agenda into the 1960s as the Brigade grappled with ways of attracting new members into the organisation, and indeed in holding onto the members they had. The Haynes Commission, under Sir George Haynes, convened to consider ways to improve the Brigade and widen its appeal. Indeed, nothing was off limits, as even the continuance of drill was under debate. As Birch wrote in his history in 1966: '"Discipline" may nowadays be a word out of fashion. Few people like being pushed around…' Thankfully, drill in moderation was maintained, but major changes were on the way.

*Left*: An early Duke of Edinburgh Award badge, as worn by a BB member.

*Below*: The 1st Fraserburgh Company wearing the 1963 uniform, including white haversack, lanyard and brown leather belt. They are also wearing the 'Thunderbird cap', which was introduced in 1970.

First, in 1963, a new full uniform was introduced. The change was necessary in order to bring in a standard full uniform. As Hurst again commented, this uniform was more expensive than the one it hoped to replace, but it would also increase smartness. The new uniform was, however, slow to roll out in some areas, with many sticking to the 'accoutrements' of cap, belt and haversack worn over normal clothing, which dated back to 1885.

The Haynes Commission also proposed a 'three-tier Brigade', which it deemed to be necessary to cater for the needs of every boy of every age group in the Brigade. This move, which was formalised in 1966, recognised a Brigade of three units. At the top there was BB Senior Section for boys aged sixteen to nineteen, beneath that the BB Company Section for Boys aged twelve to fifteen and crucially, beneath that, the Junior Section (formerly Life Boys) for boys aged seven to eleven. In most companies the seniors and regular BB boys continued to meet together but were offered different programmes, whereas the Junior Section was technically an altogether new body that was now integrated within the company.

Junior Sections would generally continue to meet separately from the older boys, and were given a new uniform: a plain navy sweatshirt with the BB badge, as well as grey shorts and socks. It also saw the end of the old sailor's hat in 1970, which was replaced with the cloth 'Thunderbirds' hat. There was now just one cap, worn by all three sections of the brigade.

A Life Boys/Junior Section team in uniform. The white lanyard around the neck denotes a leading boy in the section (*c*.1966).

The award system also changed in 1968, introducing the so-called 'barrel' badges, which, to be quite frank, looked fairly non-descript compared to the old-style badges – some of which had been used for over fifty years. In total twenty-four specialised badges were available, which brought in many of the old topics but now included canoeing, communications, drill, expedition and sailing badges, to name but a few. A brand-new President's Badge was also introduced as the second-highest award to the new-look barrel version of the Queen's Badge.

The final great change to the reorganisation of the Brigade was the introduction of a pre-Junior Section in 1976, which became the 'Anchor Boys'. The Anchor Boys cater for boys in the five to eight age range and as such operate on an entirely different level from even the Junior Section. While they do have a uniform, consisting only of a red sweatshirt and their badges, the section is obviously exempt from drill. The activities of the Anchor Boys reflect the Christian backdrop of the organisation and often give children their introduction to the Bible. Further activities consist of crafts and games. Their inclusion as part of the BB company was to hold as many boys of that age and feed them to the Junior Section before those boys might have been tempted to join other similar organisations, which may have seen them not joining the BB. By 1978 there were already 911 sections set up, consisting of 16,300 boys.

While the reorganisation of the Brigade during this period did much to grow the Brigade in both the Junior Section and the Anchor Boys, it failed to address the problems of recruitment and retention with the older sections. In 1970 the Company and Senior Sections had just over 65,000 members, compared to a peak of 92,000 members in 1960. The fault did not lie entirely with the Brigade, which stayed true to its Christian message, but with a society that was rapidly changing. The two greatest issues facing the organisation was the general decrease in church membership during the period, and the increase in other secular activities boys could participate in. Unfortunately, this was a trend that would continue into the 1980s and 1990s.

The introduction of the new cap in 1970 was the final phasing out of the forage caps used in the Brigade since the founder introduced them in 1883.

*Above*: The 1st Fraserburgh Junior Section wearing the uniform introduced in 1966 for the Junior Section. Note that the boys are wearing the same type of 'Thunderbird' hat as the Company/Senior Section. (Photograph courtesy of Andrew West)

*Right*: The Junior Section award scheme had four main themes: Spiritual, Social, Educational and Physical.

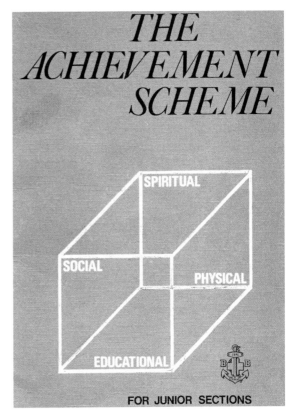

Junior Section badges as issued to boys from 1966 until around 2002.

In 1968 the Company Section award system changed, with twenty-four barrel badges being introduced to appeal to a vast range of interests. (Courtesy of Borneo Stedfast Heritage Project)

*Above left*: As part of the 1968 reorganisation of the award scheme, a new barrel badge version of the Queen's Badge was introduced, and was used until 1994.

*Above right*: The President's Badge was also introduced in 1968 as the second highest award in the organisation. The badge survives to the present day as pictured.

Introduced in 1976, the Anchor Boys continue to wear a distinctive red sweatshirt, but have never been issued with hats.

# Chapter 8

# Challenging Times

As the Boys' Brigade approached its centenary, it did so as any other mere mortal. There was a feeling that its best days were behind it, and it seemed to have fallen into an unstoppable decline. A historian of the Brigade, John Springhall, wrote: 'In the late 1970s, only a third of eighteen districts in Great Britain and Ireland managed to hold their own or show any increase in boy strength: Wales, West Lowland, North Scottish, Northern Ireland, Republic of Ireland, and the North of England.' This, he states, shows that as the centenary approached, the BB was retreating to its 'traditional geographical bases of support'.

Despite encouraging numbers from the Junior Section, and being buoyed with the creation of the Anchor Boys, the Company and Senior Sections were continuing to struggle. Between 1960 and 1982 national membership of Company Section boys had fallen from 92,000 to 53,000, while between 1968 and 1982 the number of boys in Senior Section plummeted from 3,300 to 878. The Boys' Brigade, in its tenth decade, was now clearly starting to falter. Many working groups were set up by the Executive, but, as was found with the Haynes Report, it almost always ended in a clash between the modernisers and traditionalists who lamented every change, regardless of its insignificance.

The Brigade was also struggling to recruit and retain voluntary officers and leaders in some areas, which was just as serious a problem as dropping membership. Indeed, if the officers were not there to provide an engaging programme, numbers were certain to drop. To help overcome this problem, a motion was carried at Brigade Council at Aberdeen in 1976 to allow female officers to be appointed to all sections of the Brigade. This came almost sixty years after female instructors were first approved with the introduction of the Boy Reserve in 1917. Female officers were no doubt approved mainly to help staff the new Anchor Boy Sections, which were originally almost exclusively staffed by women (although overwhelmingly labelled as 'leaders'), but they could now also serve as fully fledged officers in the Junior Section and Company Section too. Furthermore, female Company Captains also became a possibility due to this change in the rules. This move was long overdue in the BB and has been important for the organisation of today, where roughly 50 per cent of officers are women.

While the gradual introduction of equality in a male dominated organisation was perhaps one of the more positive operational changes of the 1970s, the Boys' Brigade charged forward and continued to serve its role in public life. Just as in the 1930s, the

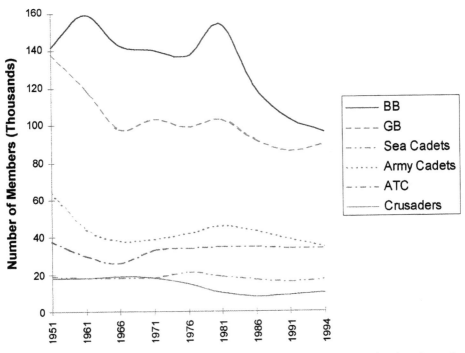

Like many youth groups, the Boys' Brigade suffered a decline in membership from the 1960s. As can be seen, the introduction of the Anchor Boys provided a lift in the mid-1970s.

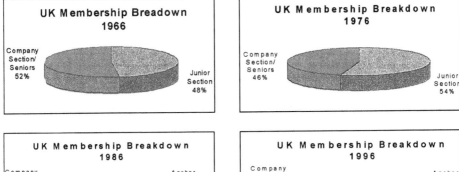

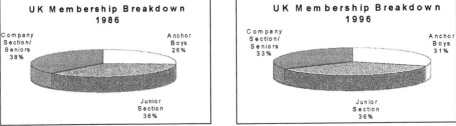

BB membership changed from being mostly teens in 1966, to being predominantly for under-elevens by 1996.

organisation used national celebrations as a means of bolstering its profile. First, in 1977, the BB celebrated the Silver Jubilee of its Patron, Queen Elizabeth II. In a tradition first set in 1937, the obligatory ceremonial badge was issued, but more unusually two badges were designed: one for England and one for Scotland. A Loyal Address was also sent to the Queen, giving thanks 'for your Majesty's twenty-five years of devoted service to the nation and the unfailing example your Majesty has given of the Christian life, which has been a constant source of encouragement to us who seek to advance Christ's Kingdom among Boys'.

The most significant celebration was, of course, for the Centenary itself in 1982/3. As would be expected the celebrations started in Glasgow, where the Brigade remained strongest. In keeping with the religious foundation of the Brigade, a thanksgiving service was presided over by the Moderator of the Church of Scotland: 'It is impossible to think back across these 100 years or to recall in memory our own years of membership of the Brigade, without measuring it largely in terms of friends and the friendships that they shared with us. This is the human face, or more accurately, the many human faces of a movement which has its divine origin in the Kingdom of Christ.'

The Centenary was an occasion for nostalgia as well as celebration, just as it had been fifty years earlier. Indeed, the casket left by the boys of 1933 was opened by the boys of 1983. It contained publications from the jubilee year, and a special message from one generation to the other:

> We the Boys of the Jubilee Session, send this Greeting across the years to you boys who will be our successors. When we write this, you are yet unborn ... We greet you all and rejoice to think that the BB spirit which is past down from generation to generation will reach you too through 50 years, and link us all in the great Comradeship of the Boys' Brigade.

Two BB badges were designed for the Silver Jubilee, one for England (left) and one for Scotland (right).

*Right*: The official commemorative badge to celebrate the Centenary in 1983.

*Below*: The official naming of Class 86 No. 86243 *The Boys' Brigade* to mark the BB centenary in 1983 by Sir David McNee.

New BB achievement badges were introduced in 1983, focusing on Interests, Physical, Community, Adventure and Leadership.

The Centenary was celebrated the length and breadth of the country and overseas, giving a boost to the organisation, which had been in the doldrums. The event was a PR success for the Brigade, which included the issuing of a BB stamp, a double-decker BB bus on publicity rounds and even the naming of a locomotive – *The Boys' Brigade*.

The Centenary year also saw more practical and long-lasting changes to the structure of the Company and Senior Sections with the introduction of a new badge structure. This had been the first big shake up since the programme since the introduction of the 1968 barrel badges, which were numerous. The new badge structure would focus on five main themes rather than twenty-six specific topics: Adventure, Leadership, Community, Interests and Physical. Boys were given more freedom in terms of what topics they undertook within these themes in a more flexible system that catered towards the boys' own individual interests. When grade three was reached on each badge (achievement of blue surrounds), the boy qualified for his President's Badge, and could then start working towards his Queen's.

# Chapter 9

# A Brigade for the Twenty-First Century

As has been demonstrated in the preceding chapters, the Boys' Brigade is an organisation that is not afraid to adapt in order to survive. Truth being told, from the 1970s and into the 2000s the Boys' Brigade risked becoming an organisation stuck in the past. More radical change was going to be necessary, not only for the Brigade to become more appealing to the youth of the twenty-first century, but also to survive.

One element in need of being updated was the Company/Senior Section uniform, which had seen no official update since 1963. The hat, haversack, lanyard and brass belt buckle had been the recognisable sign of the BB for generations, but with dropping membership it was recognised as being both old fashioned and unpopular with young people. At the Brigade Council in 1999, a motion was carried to simplify the uniform, and to have it rolled out to all companies by 2006. The change would see the end of the haversack, lanyard and brass belt. There was also an attempt to get rid of the hat, but when it became clear this would be a step too far it was dropped. Hats would now, however, be an optional accoutrement!

The official uniform would now consist of a plain blue shirt, a blue tie, and armband and badges, as well as smart shoes and trousers. A less formal uniform, consisting of a navy sweatshirt, was also approved. For many this change was a disappointment which removed the element of self-respect and pride in uniform as little care and attention to uniform would now be required in comparison to the old.

By the time the BB came to celebrate its 125th anniversary in 2008 even greater change was on the agenda. In the preceding years other youth groups had modernised by extending membership to both boys and girls as a means of boosting membership and promoting inclusiveness. It must be admitted that while other organisations like the Scouts changed, most BB officers and general commentators believed it was highly unlikely that the Boys' Brigade – as the name would suggest – would ever admit girls.

The Brigade was facing the same pressures as other (particularly) Christian organisations with falling memberships. This was doubled with pressures from equality legislation: what right did the BB have to deny girls the same opportunities it afforded to boys? Many pointed to the Girl Guides and Girls' Brigade, but even so, why should girls be excluded if they expressed an interest in the BB? Lastly, this matter of a lack of inclusion could have an impact in funding for the Brigade: applications for public money and grants tend to have more impact when those groups do not exclude 50 per cent of the youth population due to gender.

Company Section boys of the Buchan Battalion parading in the new uniforms. Some wear a shirt and tie, while some wear sweatshirts. Also note that while some have retained hats, others have not!

The Junior Section uniform also underwent a modest update in the early 2000s. As with Company/Senior sections, hats are now optional.

The Brigade Executive first proposed the idea of admitting girls to the organisation with the sanctioning of so-called 'Amicus' (mixed gender) groups for older members. In 2006 it was proposed that in cases where there was a will of the company and church, and where there was a need (e.g. if the church had no Girls' Brigade). The motion was subsequently debated at the 2007 Council at Bradford, with 58 per cent of votes cast in favour of allowing female members. This fell short of the 2/3 majority required to change the Brigade constitution. After another year of consultation and debate, the motion was approved by 280 votes to forty-eight, thereby altering the constitution. Since that vote companies have been able to apply to accept members of the Girls Association within the BB, which, much like the 1926 amalgamation, did much to aid membership in England. Over the past decade, female membership has increased in Scotland and is becoming more and more widely accepted.

Retention of young people and increasing the membership remains a priority for the Brigade and so it works tirelessly to keep the work relevant. A full-scale relaunch of the badge structure for Juniors, Company and Senior sections was completed by the time of the 125th anniversary in 2008. In August 2007 the Discover Programme was launched for the eleven to fifteen age group. It centred round the three themes of Community, Recreation and Skills: 'It's about young people learning new skills, making their own decisions and then achieving their personal goals.' A year later the Challenge Plus Programme for the fifteen to eighteen age band was launched with topics focusing on 'building life skills, encouraging recreation and leisure pursuits and being an active citizen'. An important element of both is the idea of young people making decisions for themselves and deploying early leadership skills.

Leadership potential is further enhanced within in the framework of the top Boys' Brigade awards. A leadership skills course is required before the President's Badge can be awarded, and in attaining the Queen's Badge the participant is forced to act on their initiative to ensure the requirement of the badge are met. According to the Boys' Brigade website, 982 Queen's Badges were awarded in 2014, resulting in 75,000 hours of volunteering in the community. Happily for BB members, participation in the Duke of Edinburgh Award scheme counts towards the Queen's Badge, and about 1,000 BB members participate in that programme.

Developing leadership skills and 'having a say' has been further harnessed by the Young Leaders Network, which encourages socialising among BB senior boys at fun activities outside the BB meeting. Generally speaking this group for older members is organised at battalion level, but crucially it is organised by older boys and young officers (under twenty-four). A national element of this group organises an overseas trip for young people. In addition to developing leadership skills, this group has proved successful in retaining older boys and seeing them through the transition to become officers.

The Brigade does, though, still cherish its history and will celebrate it where it is appropriate to do so. Although annual summer camps remain popular with most, the 125th anniversary of the 1st Glasgow's first camp in 2011 was used to encourage all companies around the country to participate in a camp or overnight residential. Nostalgia played its part in this campaign as when former members recall their days in the BB, the camp memories were often the best memories. The history of physical fitness is also still cherished, although many companies have now retired their gymnasts. Competition sports are the preferred activity of the twenty-first century, and so the

*Above left*: The Brigade Council approved female members in 2008. Since then many 'Queenswomen' have achieved the Queen's Badge, the BB's highest award, including Heather Doherty in 2014. (Courtesy of 7th Doncaster BB)

*Above right*: Challenge Plus is aimed at the sixteen to nineteen-year-old age group, offering greater freedom and challenges while working on the advanced badge programme. (Copyright of The Boys' Brigade)

*Left*: Recruitment literature now focuses on 'Adventure'. (Copyright of The Boys' Brigade)

Brigade offers young people a chance to come together to participate in sports and get fit in the process. This has been recognised by the government in an age where childhood obesity is a real danger to public health. In 2017 national celebrations were held across the country to commemorate 100 years of the Juniors.

All these campaigns and activities are aimed at increasing the appeal of the Brigade and boosting membership in a non-obvious fashion, but the Brigade has been honest with the membership and has launched more direct recruitment drives. In 2012, as part of 'Growing Bigger, Growing Better', every company in the country was encouraged to grow by 10 per cent. This was a relatively successful campaign, which may well have been boosted by the economic downturn. In 2016 the 'One For All' campaign was introduced, which challenges every BB section in the country to grow by at least one member. Recruitment is such a priority that recruitment badges have been introduced for the first time.

In addition to efforts in increasing membership, the current Brigade Secretary and CEO of the Boys' Brigade, Bill Stevenson, has outlined a vision of the BB, offering 'Opportunities for All': 'One of the Brigade's strengths is that young people have had the opportunity to take part in varied and exciting programmes regardless of what age groups they are attending.' The Brigade Secretary notes, however, a 'growing realisation' that not all members have access to the full range of activities offered through the BB programme. The Brigade Secretary goes on to state, 'In an attempt to address this I would suggest that we now look at challenging all companies to adopting a basic programme or collaborate with other companies/battalions to ensure all our members have the best possible BB experience.'

In the Brigade Secretary's vision, for example, every Senior BB member should have access to the Challenge Plus badge scheme, and have access to the higher badge schemes such as the President's Badge, Queen's Badge and DoE Award. Other 'musts'

Boys' Brigade Company/ Senior section badges as issued today. Badges of the Discover programme are displayed on the top row, while Challenge Plus badges are displayed in the row immediately below.

The Queen's Badge remains the highest award in the Boys' Brigade in the United Kingdom. The current design has been used since 1994.

The 125 Camping Badge. Camping has remained a popular part of the BB programme since it was introduced by the founder in 1886. (Copyright of the Boys' Brigade)

*Right*: Bill Stevenson is the current Brigade Secretary/CEO of the Boys' Brigade. (Copyright of the Boys' Brigade)

*Below*: The Boys' Brigade: The Adventure Begins Here. (Copyright of The Boys' Brigade)

would be to attend an annual summer camp, at least one overseas holiday and a major activity holiday. A basic standard for Company Section would again include camping, an opportunity to learn a musical instrument/join a band and attend at least two residentials per session. Opportunities should still be offered to the Junior Section and Anchors – the former being offered weekend camps and at least one major trip per year, with the latter being offered visits to, for example, the police and fire brigade.

It is clear, therefore, that the Boys' Brigade still has much to offer the youth of the twenty-first century, and still offers a fun and exciting programme that is attractive to young people. If the Brigade Secretary's vision is carried out successfully, and the minimum standard he promotes is implemented, it is difficult to see how the BB can fail to appeal. The principal aim of the Secretary continues to mirror that of the first Secretary and founder: to bring as many young people to Christ as possible. He has described the Boys' Brigade as being 'my ministry', a commitment highlighting the one great constant in the history of the BB.

# Conclusion

As we have seen from the pages of this short history, the Boys' Brigade has survived for over 135 years by consistently appealing to the interests of young people. Of course, through the passage of time this has required the organisation to change and develop along with the appetites of society. The majority of this book has focused on the early development of the Brigade, perhaps showing the most important transition from the strict military discipline of the founder, Sir William, in 1883, to the demilitarised, fitness-centred Brigade of his son Stanley in 1926.

We may ask ourselves the impossible question of what would the founder make of the change in direction the Brigade has taken since his death? Although the answer will never be known, we can reasonably presume that he was contented with a slight shift from strict military discipline by the additional interests adopted by the Brigade by the time of his death in 1914 – camping, first aid classes and musical proficiency, all of which continue to be part of many BB programmes today. Additionally, it should perhaps be noted that he made no criticism of battalions like Aberdeen, which prospered as promoters of physical fitness through competition, while discouraging the practice of carrying dummy rifles.

Whether or not it was his vision, there can be no doubt that the Brigade initially grew due to its transition away from militarism, reaching the peak of its influence between the 1930s and the 1960s. In addition to producing clean living and physically fit young men, this period saw the remit somewhat expand to producing useful, community-minded citizens (particularly during the Second World War). Thus, it continued even then to fulfil many of the aims of the founder in keeping young minds busy, and in keeping them out of mischief. During the same period, and despite subtle changes, the uniformed element continued to be strong and would surely have continued to impress Sir William, the 'stickler' who inspected uniforms with military precision!

As we approached the modern age, and the beginning of the decline in UK BB membership, was it and is it still practical for the Brigade to base itself on the worldview of a Victorian gentleman? The answer, of course, is no. Over the last twenty years, the UK/ROI Brigade has been forced to undergo major change in order to survive, and for that it should make no apology. It is highly doubtful that Sir William would approve of the uniform worn by most companies today, and indeed some of the activities undertaken! What of the informality? Girls in the Boys' Brigade? Some elements would now be entirely alien to his worldview and practice.

As leaders, however, we can be sure that Sir William would ultimately approve of the valuable service carried out by thousands of steadfast volunteers today; for in the

The memory of the founder lives on in the Boys' Brigade today, his birthplace at Pennyland remaining a site of pilgrimage for BB officers.

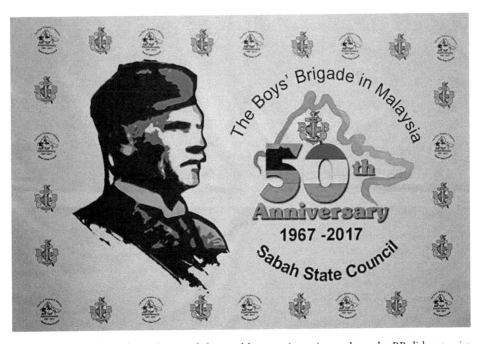

The founder is still celebrated around the world – even in regions where the BB did not exist until long after his death. (By kind permission of Sabah State Council)

While camping has remained popular since first introduced in 1886, it has increasingly become less regimented and more relaxed. These days, camps are more focused on adventure activities.

The Boys' Brigade gradually moved from militarism to an organisation based on physical fitness in the early to mid-twentieth century.

While the Brigade has changed significantly since 1883, it remains an organisation steeped in history and tradition. It does so while embracing change as it marches securely into a new century.

twenty-first century, despite all the change, the principal aim of the organisation remains the same – 'the Advancement of Christ's Kingdom'. When Sir William founded the BB in 1883, he did it as an innovative way to bring more boys to his struggling Sunday school and church. In 2018, volunteers have adapted and innovated their interpretation of the BB to do exactly the same thing in their communities.

Whatever the future holds for the Boys' Brigade, this founding principle is the only one that needs to be maintained for the organisation to preserve its identity. Everything else, from the uniform, to the activities, to the programme, is secondary to that and must change with the times to ensure that the Boys' Brigade continues to go from strength to strength into the remaining part of the twenty-first century.

# Bibliography

Birch, A. E., *The Story of the Boys' Brigade* (Muller, 1965).
Bolton, R., *Boys of the Brigade Volume One* (S. B. Publications, 1991).
Gibbon, F. P., *William A. Smith of the Boys' Brigade* (Collins, 1959).
Springhall, J., et al, *Sure and Stedfast: A History of the Boys' Brigade* (The Boys' Brigade, 1983).
*The Boys' Brigade: Retention Through the Teenage Years* (June 1997).

## Pamphlets published by the Glasgow Stedfast Association

*A Brief History of the 16th Battalion Highland Light Infantry.*
*Glasgow Battalion Minute Book (1885–96).*
Smith, W. A., *The Story of the Boys' Brigade* (First issued in 1888).
*The Boys' Brigade History of the Glasgow Battalion and notes on the Bazaar 1891* (First issued in 1891).

# Acknowledgements

The author wishes to acknowledge and thank John Cooper of Glasgow Battalion, M. Lu of the Borneo Stedfast Heritage Project, and published BB author Robin Bolton for the help and advice given in the production of this illustrated history. The author further wishes to thank The Boys' Brigade for the use of logos.